Above. Blarney Castle, County Cork

THOUSAND YEARS OF IRISH POETRY

*The living tradition – from pagan times to the voices
of the twenty-first century*

—— *Edited by Andrew Pagett* ——

CAXTON EDITIONS

First published in Great Britain in 2001 by Caxton Editions
A member of the Caxton Publishing Group
20 Bloomsbury Street
London WC1B 3QA

© Caxton Editions, 2001

ISBN 1 84067 147 5

Designed and produced for Caxton Editions
by Savitri Books Ltd

ACKNOWLEDGEMENTS

Permission to use copyright material is gratefully acknowledged to the following: The poems
by W.B. Yeats are reprinted with the permission of A P Watt and of Scribner, a Division of
Simon & Schuster from the COLLECTED POEMS OF W.B YEATS, Revised Second Edition edited by
Richard J. Finneran (New York: Scribner, 1996; Society of Authors for the poem by James
Joyce; David Higham Associates for poem by Louis MacNeice; the two poems by Patrick
Kavanagh are reprinted by permission of Peter Kavanagh from THE COMPLETE POEMS OF
PATRICK KAVANAGH, New York, 1966, edited and with commentary by Peter Kavanagh.;
Carcanet Press Limited for the poems by Thomas Kinsella; the poem by John Montague from
COLLECTED POEMS (1995) is reproduced by kind permission of the author and The Gallery
Press and by Wake Forest University Press; Bloodaxe Publishers and the author for poems by
Brendan Kennelly; 'The Follower', 'The Forge' and 'The Rain Stick' from OPENED GROUND:
SELECTED POEMS 1966-1996 by Seamus Heaney. Copyright © 1998 by Seamus Heaney.
Reprinted by permission of Faber and Faber and of Farrar, Straus & Giroux, LLC. Every effort
has been made to trace the copyright holders. The editor apologizes for any omission which
may have occurred.

OUR HERITAGE

This heritage to the race of Kings:

Their children and their children's seed

Have wrought their prophecies in deed

Of terrible and splendid things.

The hands that fought, the hearts that broke

In old immortal tragedies,

These have not failed beneath the skies,

Their children's heads refuse the yoke.

And still their hands shall guard the sod

That holds their father's funeral urn,

Still shall their hearts volcanic burn

With anger of the Sons of God.

No alien sword shall earn as wage

The entail of their blood and tears,

No shameful price for peaceful years

Shall ever part this heritage.

Joseph Mary Plunkett *(1887–1916)*

Above. The Round Tower and Abbey, Devenish Isle

INTRODUCTION

From earliest times to present day, poetry and poets have held a special place in the Irish psyche. The arrival of St. Patrick in 432 was to determine the religious and cultural destiny of Ireland. Irish history was then punctuated by successive invasions starting with the Vikings around 794, the Normans around 1170 and culminating with the arrival of the English around 1270. These events brought much destruction and misery but also a wealth of languages and cultural influences ranging from Latin, Norse, French and, of course, English. These various strands fused with the prevailing Gaelic and, out of this melting pot, emerged Irish culture and literature as we know it today. The process of the forced introduction of English was a painful one: Irishmen were banned from speaking or writing Gaelic under threat of death.

Whereas many other peoples would have been, if not silenced at least handicapped, by the banning of their own language and by being forced to accept a foreign idiom as their means of everyday as well as of cultural expression and form of communication, the Irish turned the situation to their advantage. Like the sorcerer's apprentice, they not only made the English language their own, but became some of its best exponents, displaying an unmatched verbal virtuosity and richness of expression. This means, however, that a huge slice of Irish writings is inaccessible, not only to an international audience, but also to many Irish readers who do not speak Gaelic. It was important to show the unbroken tradition which links the writings of Seamus

Heaney and of other modern Irish poets with the earliest Gaelic texts, such as the writings of Torna, for instance, and to make these wonders from the distant past known to a popular readership, albeit in English translation.

Of course, the very size of the enterprise inevitably means that there will be gaps in the representation of a thousand years of Irish poetry and that, as in all anthologies, the compilers can only hope to give a taste of the wealth of material available. It is hoped, however, that the present collection will give readers the incentive to look for the works of other Irish poets, ancient and modern, or to read other poems by the writers represented in this volume.

The beauty of Alfred Heaton Cooper's illustrations makes them a fitting tribute to the words and convey the timeless charm of the landscapes which inspired and sustained Ireland's poets through the dark and turbulent years.

Below. Killiney Hill and Bay

TORNA

(Attributed, Torna, was the last great bard of Pagan Ireland. He died some time in the 5th Century.) Among the poems by him that have reached us is this lament over Corc and Niall of the Nine Hostages, who had fostered him in childhood.

My foster children were not slack;

Corc or Niall ne'er turned his back:

Niall, of Tara's palace hoar,

Worthy seed of Owen More;

Corc, of Cashel's pleasant rock,

Con-cead-caha's (*) honoured stock.

Joint exploits made Erin theirs—

Joint exploits of high compeers;

Fierce they were, and stormy strong;

Niall, amid the reeling throng,

Stood terrific; nor was Corc

Hindmost in the heavy work.

Niall Mac Eochy Vivahain

Ravaged Albin, hill and plain;

While he fought from Tara far,

Corc disdained unequal war.

Never saw I man like Niall,

Making foreign foemen reel;

Never saw I man like Corc,

Swinging at the savage work;

Never saw I better twain,

Search all Erin round again—

Twain so stout in warlike deeds—

Twain so mild in peaceful weeds.

These the foster-children swain

Of Torna, I who sing the strain;

These they are, the pious ones,

My sons, my darling foster-sonsl

Who duly every day would come

To glad the old man's lonely home.

Ah, happy days I've spent between

Old Tara's hall and Cashel-green!

From Tara down to Cashel ford,

From Cashel back to Tara's lord.

When with Niall, his regent, I

Dealt with princes royally.

If with Corc perchance I were,

I was his prime counsellor.

Therefore Niall I ever set

On my right hand—thus to get

Judgements grave, and weighty words,

Right. Glengariff

For the right hand loyal lords;

But, ever on my left-hand side,

Gentle Corc, who knew not pride,

That none other so might part

His dear body from my heart.

Gone is generous Corc O'Yeon—woe is me!

Gone is valiant Niall O'Con—woe is me!

Gone the root of Tara's stock—woe is me!

Gone the head of Cashel rock—woe is me!

Broken is my witless brain—

Niall, the mighty king, is slain!

Broken is my bruised heart's core—

Corc, the Righ-More (**), is no more!

Mourns Lea Con, in tribute's chain,

Lost Mac Eochy Vivahain,

And her lost Mac Lewy true—

Mourns Lea Mogha (***), ruined too!

Translated by Samuel Ferguson

* Con-cead-caha: King Conn of the Hundred Battles

** Righ-More; Great King

*** Circa A.D. 180, under the reign of King Conn of the Hundred Battles, Ireland became divided in two parts: Lea Mogha and Leath Mogha. The princes Corc and Niall were the ambassadors of these two provinces.

Anonymous *(8th or early 9th century) A marginal poem on Codex S. Pauli,
by a student of the Monastery of Carinthia*

THE MONK AND HIS PET CAT

I and my white cat Pangur

Each has his special art;

His mind is set on hunting mice

Mine on my special craft.

Better than fame I love to rest

With close study of my beloved book;

White Pangur does not envy me,

He loves to ply his childish games.

When we two are alone in our house

It is a tale without tedium;

Each of us has games never ending

Something to sharpen our wit upon.

At times by feats of valour

A mouse sticks in his net,

While into my net there drops

A loved law of obscure meaning.

His eye, this flashing full one,

He points against the fence wall

While against the fine edge of science

I point my clear but feeble eye.

He is joyous with swift jumping

When a mouse sticks in his sharp claw,

And I too am joyous when I have grasped

The elusive but well loved problem.

Though we thus play at all times

Neither hinders the other –

each is happy with his own art,

Pursues it with delight.

He is master of the work

Which he does every day

While I am master of my work,

Bringing to obscure laws clarity.

This version of the poem is based on

translations by Whitley Stokes, John Strachan,

and Kuno Meyer

Right. Innisfallen Island, Killarney

St. Colman *(attributed, 8th century)*

HYMN AGAINST PESTILENCE

God's blessing lead us, help us!

May Mary's Son veil us!

May we be under His safeguard to-night!

Whither we go may He guard us well!

Whether in rest or motion,

Whether sitting or standing,

The Lord of Heaven against every strife,

This is the prayer that we will pray.

May the prayer of Abel son of Adam,

Enoch, Elias help us;

May they save us from swift disease

On whatever side, throughout the noisy world.

Noah and Abraham,

Isaac the wonderful son,

May they surround us against pestilence,

That famine may not come to us!

We entreat the father of three tetrads,

And Joseph their junior:

May their prayers save us

To the King many-angeled, noblel

May Moses the good leader protect us,

Who protected us through Rubrum Mare,

David the bold lad.

May Job with his trials

Protect us past the poisons!

May God's prophets defend us,

With Maccabee's seven sons!

John the Baptist we invoke,

May he be a safeguard to us, a protection!

May Jesus with His apostles

Be for our help against danger!

Translated by Whitley Stokes and John Strachan

Anonymous *(8th century)*

THE HOLY MAN

He is a bird round which a trap closes,

He is a leaky ship to which peril is dangerous,

He is an empty vessel, he is a withered tree,

Whoso doth not the will of the King above.

He is pure gold, he is the radiance round the sun,

He is a vessel of silver with wine,

He is happy, is beautiful, is holy,

Whoso doth the will of the King.

Translated by Whitley Stokes and John Strachan

Ninine *(8th century)*

PRAYER TO ST. PATRICK

We invoke holy Patrick, Ireland's chief apostle.

Glorious is his wondrous name, a flame that baptized heathen;

He warred against hard-hearted wizards.

He thrust down the proud with the help of our Lord of fair heaven.

He purified Ireland's meadow-lands, a mighty birth.

We pray to Patrick chief apostle; his judgment hath delivered

us in Doom from the malevolence of dark devils.

God be with us, together with the prayer of Patrick, chief apostle.

Translated by Whitley Stokes and John Strachan

Below. Mirror of the morning sky, Killery Harbour

St. Patrick *(attributed. 9th century)*

GOD'S BLESSING ON MUNSTER

God's blessing on Munster

Men, boys, women!

Blessing on the land

That gives them fruit!

Blessing on every treasure

That shall be produced on their plains,

Without anyone in want of help,

God's blessing on Munster!

Blessing on their peaks,

On their bare flagstones,

Blessing on their glens,

Blessing on their ridges.

Like sand of sea under ships,

Be the number of their hearths:

On slopes, on plains, On mountains, or peaks.

Translated by Whitley Stokes

Anonymous *(probably 9th century)*

THE SCRIBE

Around me a strand of trees:

A blackbird sings to me.

From above my beloved book,

Sing the birds, to me.

The grey-cloaked cuckoo chants to me

From his perch over the bush.

May the Lord protect me from despair

As I write, happy, under the greening of the trees.

New arrangement by A.P.

Anonymous *(9th century)*

SUMMER IS GONE

My tidings for you: the stag bells,

Winter snows, summer is gone.

Wind high and cold, low the sun,

Short his course, sea running high.

Deep-red the bracken, its shape all gone—

The wild-goose has raised his wonted cry.

Cold has caught the wings of birds;

Season of ice – these are my tidings.

❧❧

Anonymous *(10th century)*

A SONG OF WINTER

Cold, cold!

Cold tonight is broad Moylurg.

Higher the snow than the mountain-range,

The deer cannot get at their food.

Cold till Doom!

The storm has spread over all:

A river is each furrow upon the slope,

Each ford a full pool.

A great tidal sea is each loch,

A full loch is each pool:

Horses cannot get over the ford of Ross,

No more can two feet get there.

The wolves of Cuan-wood get

Neither rest nor sleep in their lair,

The little wren cannot find

Shelter in her nest on the slope of Lon.

Keen wind and cold ice

Has burst upon the little company of birds,

Below. Mount Errigal, Gweedore, County Donnegal

The blackbird cannot get a lee to her liking,

Shelter for its side in Cuan-wood.

Cosy our pot on its hook,

Crazy the hut on the slope of Lon:

The snow has crushed the wood here,

Toilsome to climb up Ben-bo.

From flock and from dawn to rise –

Take it to heart! – were folly for thee:

Ice in heaps on every ford –

That is why I say 'cold'!

(extract) translated by Kuno Meyer

Cormac *(Cormac, who was the King-Bishop of Cashel lived from 837-903and was regarded as one of the most distinguished scholars of his period. The poem reproduced overleaf comes from his* Book of Leinster.*)*

THE HEAVENLY PILOT

Wilt Thou steer my frail black bark

O'er the dark broad ocean's foam?

Wilt Thou come, Lord, to my boat,

Where afloat, my will would roam?

Thine the mighty: Thine the small:

Thine to mark men fall, like rain;

God! wilt Thou grant aid to me

Who came o'er th' upheaving main?

Translated by George Sigerson

Anonymous *(10th century)*

EVE'S LAMENT

I am Eve, great Adam's wife,

'Tis I that outraged Jesus of old;

'Tis I that robbed my children of Heaven,

By right 'tis I that should have gone upon the cross.

I had a kingly house to please me,

Grievous the evil choice that disgraced me,

Grievous the wicked advice that withered me!

Alas! my hand is not pure.

'Tis I that plucked the apple,

Which went across my gullet:

So long as they endure in the light of day,

So long women will not cease from folly.

There would be no ice in any place,

There would be no glistening windy winter,

There would be no hell, there would be no sorrow,

There would be no fear, if it were not for me.

❦❦

Mythological Cycle

THE SEA-GOD'S ADDRESS TO BRAN

Manannan the Sea-God fills a very important part in Irish legends. He is the King of the Land of Promise, sometimes known as Magh Mell or Tir na n-Og. The poem reproduced on page 30 was probably written down in the eight or even in the seventh century. It is one of the anonymous Imramba *or voyages in the* Book of Leinster. *In the story Bran went to sea. When he had been at sea for two days and two nights, he saw a man in a chariot coming towards him over the sea. It was Manannan Mac Lir (the Ocean God), who the sang these quatrains to him.*

Above. Ross Castle, Killarney

To Bran in his coracle it seems

A marvellous beauty across the clear sea:

To me in my chariot from afar

It is a flowery plain on which he rides.

What is clear sea

For the prowed skiff in which Bran is,

That to me in my chariot of two wheels

Is a delightful plain with a wealth of flowers.

Bran sees

A mass of waves beating across the clear sea:

I see myself in the Plain of Sports,

Red-headed flowers that have no flaw.

Sea-horses glisten in summer

As far as Bran can stretch his glance:

Rivers pour forth a stream of honey

In the land of Manannan, son of Ler.

The sheen of the main on which thou art,

The dazzling white of the sea on which thou rowest about

Yellow and azure are spread out,

It is a light and airy land.

Speckled salmon leap from the womb

Out of the white sea on which thou lookest:

They are calves, they are lambs of fair hue,

With truce, without mutual slaughter.

Though thou seest but one chariot-rider

In the Pleasant Plain of many flowers,

There are many steeds on its surface,

Though thou dost not see them.

Large is the plain, numerous is the host,

Colours shine with pure glory:

A white stream of silver, stairs of gold

Afford a welcome with all abundance.

An enchanting game, most delicious,

They play over the luscious wine:

Men and gentle women under a bush

Without sin, without transgression.

Along the top of a wood

Thy coracle has swum across ridges:

There is a wood laden with beautiful fruit

Under the prow of thy little skiff.

A wood with blossom and with fruit

On which is the vine's veritable fragrance,

A wood without decay, without defect,

On which is foliage of golden hue.

From the beginning of creation we are

Without old age, without consummation of clay:

Hence we expect not there should be frailty—

The sin has not come to us.

An evil day when the serpent came

To the father into his citadell

He has perverted the ages in this world,

So that there came decay which was not original.

By greed and lust he has slain us,

Whereby he has ruined his noble race:

The withered body has gone to the fold of torment,

An everlasting abode of torture.

It is a law of pride in this world

To believe in the creatures, to forget God:

Overthrow by diseases, and old age,

Destruction of the beguiled soul.

A noble salvation will come

From the King who has created us:

A white law will come over seas—

Besides being God, He will be man.

Steadily then let Bran row!

It is not far to the Land of Women:

Below. The Twelve Pins, Connemara

Evna with manifold bounteousness

He will reach before the sun is set.

Anonymous *(probably 12th century)*

THE CHURCH BELL AT NIGHT

Sweet little bell, struck on a windy night,

I would liefer keep tryst with thee

Than be

With a woman foolish and light.

Translated by Howard Mumford Jones

Anonymous *(12th century)*

ON THE DEFEAT OF RAGNALL BY MURROUGH, KING OF LEINSTER, A.D. 994

Ye people of great Murrough,

Against whom neither forest nor wild moor prevails,

Ye that before your Norse battle-standards of sunbright satin

Have routed the heathen hordes as far as the Boyne!

Blood breaks like snowflakes from their noses

As they flee across Aughty in the late evening.

Translated by Kuno Meyer

Anonymous

THE LAMENT OF MAEV LEITH-DHERG

The Maev of the poem is not the warrior-goddess of legends but

a Queen of Ireland in times approaching the historic: ca AD20.

Raise the Cromlech high!

MacMoghcorb (the charriot hound) is slain,

And other men's renown

Has leave to live again.

Cold at last he lies

Neath the burial-stone;

All the blood he shed

Could not save his own.

Stately-strong he went,

Through his nobles all

When we paced together

Up the banquet-hall.

Dazzling white as lime

Was his body fair,

Cherry-red his cheeks,

Raven-black his hair.

Razor-sharp his spear,

And the shield he bore,

High as champion's head_

His arm was like an oar.

Never aught but truth

Spake my noble king;

Valour all his trust

In all his warfaring.

As the forked pole

Holds the roof-tree's weight,

So my hero's arm

Held the battle straight.

Terror went before him,

Death behind his back;

Above. Holy Cross Abbey, Thurles, County Tipperary

Well the wolves of Erinn

Knew his chariot's track.

Seven bloody battles

He broke upon his foes;

In each a hundred heroes

Fell beneath his blows.

Once he fought at Fossud

Thrice at Ath-finn-Fail

'Twas my king that conquered

At bloody Ath-an-Scail.

At the boundary Stream

Fought the Royal Hound,

And for Bernas battle

Stands his name renowned.

Here he fought with Leinster—

Last of all his frays—

On the Hill of Cucorb's Fate

High his Cromlech raise.

Translated by T. W. Rolleston

MacConglinne *(12th century)*

A VISION THAT APPEARED TO ME

This twelfth-century vision of a paradise inhabited by gluttons of magnificent

proportions makes the poet into a true predecessor of Rabelais.

A vision that appeared to me,

An apparition wonderful

I tell to all:

There was a coracle all of lard

Within a port of New-milk Lake

Upon the world's smooth sea.

We went into that man-of-war,

'Twas warrior-like to take the road

O'er ocean's heaving waves.

Our oar-strokes then we pulled

Across the level of the main,

Throwing the sea's harvest up

Like honey, the sea-soil.

The fort we reached was beautiful,

With works of custards thick,

Beyond the lake.

Fresh butter was the bridge in front,

The rubble dyke was fair white wheat,

Bacon the palisade.

Stately, pleasantly it sat,

A compact house and strong.

Then I went in:

The door of it was hung beef,

The threshold was dry bread,

Cheese-curds the walls.

Smooth pillars of old cheese

And sappy bacon props

Alternate ranged;

Stately beams of mellow cream,

White posts of real curds

Kept up the house.

Behind it was a well of wine,

Beer and bragget in streams,

Each full pool to the taste.

Malt in smooth wavy sea

Over a lard-spring's brink

Flowed through the floor.

A lake of juicy pottage

Under a cream of oozy lard

Lay twixt it and the sea.

Hedges of butter fenced it round,

Under a crest of white-mantled lard

Around the wall outside.

Below. Cottage by the sea

A row of fragrant apple-trees,

An orchard in its pink-tipped bloom,

Between it and the hill.

A forest tall of real leeks,

Of onions and of carrots, stood

Behind the house.

Within, a household generous,

A welcome of red, firm-fed men,

Around the fire:

Seven bead-strings and necklets seven

Of cheeses and of bits of tripe

Round each man's neck.

The Chief in cloak of beefy fat

Beside his noble wife and fair

I then beheld.

Below the lofty caldron's spit

Then the Dispenser I beheld,

His fleshfork on his back.

Anonymous (12th century)

THE BLACKBIRD

Ah, blackbird, thou art satisfied

Where thy nest is in the bush:

Hermit that clinkest no bell,

Sweet, soft, peaceful is thy note.

Columcille *(attributed, 12th century)*

COLUMCILLE'S GREETING TO IRELAND

Delightful to be on the Hill of Howth

Before going over the white-haired sea:

The dashing of the wave against its face,

The bareness of its shores and of its border.

Delightful to be on the Hill of Howth

After coming over the white-bosomed sea;

To be rowing one's little coracle,

Ochone! on the wild-waved shore.

Great is the speed of my coracle,

And its stern turned upon Derry

Grievous is my errand over the main,

Travelling to Alba of the ravens.

My foot in my tuneful coracle,

My sad heart still bleeding;

A man without guidance is weak,

Blind are all the ignorant.

There is a grey eye

That will look back upon Erin:

It shall never see again

The men of Erin nor her women.

I stretch my glance across the brine

From the firm oaken planks:

Many are the tears of my soft grey eye

As I look back upon Erin.

My mind is upon Erin,

Upon Loch Lene, upon Linny,

Upon the land where Ulstermen are,

Upon gentle Munster and upon Meath.

Gael! Gael! beloved name!

It gladdens the heart to invoke it:

Beloved is Cummin of the bright hair,

Beloved are Cainnech and Comgall.

Were all Alba mine

From its centre to its border,

I would rather have the site of a house

In the middle of fair Derry.

Below. Croag Patrick and Clew Bay, Westford, County Galway

It is for this I love Derry,

For its quietness, for its purity;

All full of angels

Is every leaf on the oaks of Derry.

My Derry, my little oak-grove,

My dwelling and my little cell,

O eternal God in Heaven above,

Woe to him who violates itl

Beloved are Durrow and Derry,

Beloved is Raphoe in purity,

Beloved Drumhome of rich fruits;

Beloved are Swords and Kells.

Beloved also to my heart in the West

Drumcliff on Culcinne's strand:

To gaze upon fair Loch Foyle –

The shape of its shores is delightful.

Delightful is that, and delightful

The salt main where the sea-gulls cry,

On my coming from Derry afar,

It is quiet and it is delightful.

Delightful.

Anonymous *(12th century)*

THE CRUCIFIXION

At the cry of the first bird

They began to crucify Thee, O Swan!

Never shall lament cease because of that.

It was like the parting of day from night.

Ah, sore was the suffering borne

By the body of Mary's Son, But sorer still to Him was the grief

Which for His sake

Came upon His mother.

Translated by Howard Mumford Jones

Anonymous *(13th century)*

The minstrel of the court of the King of Spain recites the following lay as the court
awaits the arrival of Eoghan Mor who comes to ask for the hand of the King of Spain's
daughter, Momera (or Beara). Eoghan Mor, King of Munster in the second century, was
a rival of Conn of The Hundred Battles.

I HEAR THE WAVE

I hear the wave clamour from the shore,

The sound is an omen, – the harbinger of a king,

This king who comes across the green sea,

Shall by his valour take Erinn to himself.

Eoghan is the man, great shall be his triumph,

He shall hold sway over noble Erinn,

A chief of chiefs is the scion who comes over the waters;

You shall be the wife of Eoghan the strong.

This strand below is Eibhear's cold strand,

I understand the shore when I hear its sound.

Translated by Eugene O'Curry

Opposite. Rostrevor, County Down

Anonymous *(12th century)*

AN EVIL WORLD

An evil world is now at hand:

In which men shall be in bondage, women free;

Mast wanting, woods smooth, blossom bad;

Winds many, wet summer, green corn;

Much cattle, scant milk;

Dependants burdensome in every country!

Hogs lean, chiefs wicked;

Bad faith, chronic killings:

A world withered, graves in number.

Translated by Standish Hayes O'Grady

Fearflatha O'Gnive (*flourished 1562*)

THE DOWNFALL OF THE GAEL

My heart is in woe,

And my soul deep in trouble –

For the mighty are low,

And abased are the noble:

The sons of the Gael

Are in exile and mourning,

Worn, weary, and pale,

As spent pilgrims returning.

Or men who, in flight

From the field of disaster,

Beseech the black night

On their flight to fall faster;

Our course is fear,

Our nobility vileness,

Our hope is despair,

And our comeliness foulness.

There is mist on our heads,

And a cloud chill and hoary

Of black sorrow, sheds

An eclipse on our glory.

From Boyne to the Linn

Has the mandate been given,

That the children of Finn

From their country be driven.

That the sons of the king—

Oh, the treason and malice!—

Shall no more ride the ring

In their own native valleys;

No more shall repair

Where the hill foxes tarry,

Nor forth to the air

Fling the hawk at her quarry;

For the plain shall be broke

By the share of the stranger,

And the stone-mason's stroke

Tell the woods of their danger;

The green hills and shore

Be with white keeps disfigured,

And the Mote of Rathmore

Be the Saxon churl's haggard!

The land of the lakes

Shall no more know the prospect

Of valleys and brakes –

So transformed is her aspect!

The Gael cannot tell,

In the uprooted wildwood

And red ridgy dell,

The old nurse of his childhood:

The nurse of his youth

Is in doubt as she views him,

If the wan wretch, in truth,

Be the child of her bosom.

We starve by the board,

And we thirst amid wassail –

For the guest is the lord,

And the host is the vassal!

Through the woods let us roam,

Through the wastes wild and barren;

We are strangers at home!

Below. Turf pickers, Connemara

We are exiles in Erin!

And Erin's a bark

O'er the wide waters driven!

And the tempest howls dark,

And her side planks are riven!

And in billows of might

Swell the Saxon before her,—

Unite, oh, unite!

Or the billows burst o'er her!

Owen Roe Mac Ward *(attributed, 16th century)*

DARK ROSALEEN

O, my Dark Rosaleen,

Do not sigh, do not weep!

The priests are on the ocean green,

They march along the Deep.

There's wine ... from the royal Pope,

Upon the ocean green;

And spanish ale shall give you hope,

Above. Clonmacnoise, County Roscommon

My Dark Rosaleen!

My own Rosaleen!

Shall glad your heart, shall give you hope,

Shall give you health, and help, and hope,

My Dark Rosaleen!

Over hills, and through dales,

Have I roamed for your sake;

All yesterday I sailed with sails

On river and on lake.

The Erne,. at its highest flood,

I dashed across unseen,

For there was lightning in my blood,

My Dark Rosaleenl

My own Rosaleenl

Oh! there was lightning in my blood,

Red lightning lightened through my blood,

My Dark Rosaleen!

All day long, in unrest, To and fro, do I move.

You'll pray for me, my flower of flowers,

My Dark Rosaleen!

My fond Rosaleen!

You'll think of me through Daylight's hours,

My virgin flower, my flower of flowers,

My Dark Rosaleen!

I could scale the blue air,

I could plough the high hills,

Oh, I could kneel all night in prayer,

To heal your many ills!

And one ... beamy smile from you

Would float like light between

My toils and me, my own, my true,

My Dark Rosaleen!

My fond Rosaleen!

Would give me life and soul anew,

A second life, a soul anew,

My dark Rosaleen!

0! the Erne shall run red

With redundance of blood,

The earth shall rock beneath our tread,

And flames wrap hill and wood,

And gun-peal, and slogan cry,

Wake many a glen serene.

Ere you shall fade, ere you shall die,

My Dark Rosaleen!

My own Rosaleen!

The Judgement Hour must first be nigh,

Ere you can fade, ere you can die,

My Dark Rosaleen!

Translated by James Clarence Mangan

❧❧

Maurice O'Dugan (*flourished 1641*)

THE COOLUN

O had you seen the Coolun,

Walking down by the cuckoo's street,

With the dew of the meadow shining

On her milk-white twinkling feet!

My love she is, and my coleen oge,

And she dwells in Bal'nagar;

And she bears the palm of beauty bright,

From the fairest that in Erin are.

In Bal'nagar is the Coolun,

Like the berry on the bough her cheek;

Bright beauty dwells for ever

On her fair neck and ringlets sleek;

Oh, sweeter is her mouth's soft music

Than the lark or thrush at dawn,

Or the blackbird in the greenwood singing

Farewell to the setting sun.

Rise up, my boy! make ready

My horse, for I forth would ride,

Below. The village of Roundstone, County Galway

To follow the modest damsel,

Where she walks on the green hillside:

For ever since our youth were we plighted,

In faith, troth, and wedlock true—

She is sweeter to me nine times over,

Than organ or cuckoo!

For, ever since my childhood

For, ever since my childhood

I loved the fair and darling child;

But our people came between us,

And with lucre our pure love defiled:

Ah, my woe it is, and my bitter pain,

And I weep it night and day,

That the coleen bawn of my early love

Is torn from my heart away.

Sweetheart and faithful treasure,

Be constant still, and true;

Nor for want of herds and houses

Leave one who would ne'er leave you.

I'll pledge you the blessed Bible,

Without and eke within,

That the faithful God will provide for us,

Without thanks to kith or kin.

Oh, love, do you remember

When we lay all night alone,

Beneath the ash in the winter storm,

When the oak wood round did groan?

No shelter then from the blast had we,

No shelter then from the blast had we,

The bitter blast or sleet,

But your gown to wrap about our heads,

And my coat around our feet.

Translated by Samuel Ferguson

Edmond O'Ryan *(17th century)*

AH! WHAT WOES ARE MINE

Ah! what woes are mine to bear,

Life's fair morn with clouds o'ercasting!

Doomed the victim of despair!

Youth's gay bloom, pale sorrow blasting!

Sad the bird that sings alone,

Flies to wilds, unseen to languish,

Pours, unheard, the ceaseless moan,

And wastes on desert air its anguish!

Mine, O hapless bird! thy fate –

The plundered nest, – the lonely sorrow! –

The lost – loved – harmonious mate!–

The wailing night, – the cheerless morrow!

O thou dear hoard of treasured love!

Though these fond arms should ne'er possess thee,

Still – still my heart its faith shall prove,

And its last sighs shall breathe to bless thee

Translated by Charlotte Brooke

Geoffrey Keating (1570? – 1646?)

O WOMAN FULL OF WILE

O woman full of wile,

Keep from me thy hand:

I am not a man of the flesh,

Tho' thou be sick for my love.

See how my hair is grey!

See how my body is powerless!

See how my blood hath ebbed!

For what is thy desire?

Do not think me besotted:

Below. Letterfrack, Connemara

Bend not again thy head,

Let our love be without act

Forever, O slender witch.

Take thy mouth from my mouth,

Graver the matter so;

Let us not be skin to skin:

From heat cometh will.

'Tis thy curling ringleted hair,

Thy grey eye bright as dew,

Thy lovely round white breast,

That draw the desire of eyes.

Every deed but the deed of the flesh

And to lie in thy bed of sleep

Would I do for thy love,

O woman full of wile!

Translated by Padraic Pearse

Anonymous *(17th century)*

DO YOU REMEMBER THAT NIGHT?

Do you remember that night

When you were at the window,

With neither hat nor gloves

Nor coat to shelter you?

I reached out my hand to you,

And you ardently grasped it,

I remained to converse with you

Until the lark began to sing.

Do you remember that night

That you and I were

At the foot of the rowan-tree,

And the night driiting snow?

Your head on my breast,

And your pipe sweetly playing?

Little thought I that night

That our love ties would loosen!

Beloved of my inmost heart,

Come some night, and soon,

When my people are at rest,

That we may talk together.

My arms shall encircle you

While I relate my sad tale,

That your soft, pleasant converse

Hath deprived me of heaven.

The fire is unraked,

The light is unextinguished,

The key under the door,

Do you softly draw it.

My mother is asleep,

But I am wide awake;

My fortune in my hand,

I am ready to go with you.

Translated by EugeneO'Curry

Thomas Flawell *(Attributed. Late 17th century)*

THE COUNTY OF MAYO

On the deck of Patrick Lynch's boat I sat in woeful plight,

Through my sighing all the weary day and weeping all the night.

Were it not that full of sorrow from my people forth I go,

By the blessed sun, 'tis royally I'd sing thy praise, Mayo.

When I dwelt at home in plenty, and my gold did much abound,

In the company of fair young maids the Spanish ale went round.

'Tis a bitter change from those gay days that now I'm forced to go,

And must leave my bones in Santa Cruz, far from my own Mayo.

Below. A coming storm, Bertragboy Bay

'T'is my grief that patrick Loughlin is not Earl in Irrul still,

and that Brian Duff no longer rules as Lord upon the Hill;

And that Colonel Hugh Mac Grady should be lying dead and low.

And I sailing, sailing swiftly from the country of Mayo.

Extract. Translated by George Fox

Anonymous *(18th century)*

THE DAWNING OF THE DAY

At early dawn I once had been

Where Lene's blue waters flow,

When summer bid the groves be green,

The lamp of light to glow.

As on by bower, and town, and tower,

And widespread fields I stray,

I met a maid in the greenwood shade

At the dawning of the day.

Her feet and beauteous head were bare,

No mantle fair she wore;

But down her waist fell golden hair,

That swept the tall grass o'er.

With milking-pail she sought the vale

And bright her charms' display;

Outshining far the morning star

At the dawning of the day.

Beside me sat that maid divine

Where grassy banks outspread.

'Oh, let me call thee ever mine,

Dear maid,' I sportive said.

'False man, for shame, why bring me blame?'

She cried, and burst away –

The sun's first light pursued her flight

At the dawning of the day.

Translated by Edward Walsh

Turlough Carolan *(1670-1738)*

THE CUP OF O'HARA

Were I west in green Arran,

Or south in Glanmore,

Where the long ships come laden

With claret in store;

Yet I'd rather than shiploads

Of claret, and ships,

Have your white cup, O'Hara,

Up full at my lips.

But why seek in numbers

Its virtues to tell,

When O'Hara's own chaplain

Has said, saying well,—

"Turlough, bold son of Brian,

Sit ye down, boy again,

Till we drain the great cupaun

In another health to Keane."

Translated by Samuel Ferguson

Anonymous *(18th century)*

PEARL OF THE WHITE BREAST

There's a colleen fair as May,

For a year and for a day

I've sought by every way – Her heart to gain.

There's no art of tongue or eye,

Fond youths with maidens try,

But I've tried with ceaseless sigh – Yet tried in vain.

If to France or far-off Spain,

She'd cross the watery main,

Below. Cathedral Cliffs, Achill Island

To see her face again – The sea I'd brave.

And if 't is Heaven's decree,

That mine she may not be,

May the Son of Mary me – In mercy save!

Extract. *Translated by George Petrie*

Anonymous *(18th century)*

THE OUTLAW OF LOCH LENE

Oh, many a day have I made good ale in the glen.

That came not of stream, or malt, like the brewing of men;

My bed was the ground; my roof the greenwood above,

And the wealth that I sought—one far kind glance from my love.

Alas! on the night when the horses I drove from the field,

That I was not near, from terror my angel to shield!

She stretched forth her arms – her mantle she flung to the wind,

And swam o'er Loch Lene, her outlawed lover to find.

Oh, would that a freezing, sleet-winged tempest did sweep,

And I and my love were alone far off on the deep!

I'd ask not a ship, or a bark, or pinnace to save –

With her hand round my waist, I'd fear not the wind or the wave.

'Tis down by the lake where the wild tree fringes its sides,

The maid of my heart, the fair one of heaven resides:

I think, as at eve she wanders its mazes along,

The birds go to sleep by the sweet wild twist of her song.

Translated by J. J. Callanan

Anonymous *(18th century)*

THE GIRL I LOVE

The girl I love is comely, straight, and tall,

Down her white neck her auburn tresses fall;

Her dress is neat, her carriage light and free –

Here's a health to that charming maid, who e'er she be!

The rose's blush but fades beside her cheek,

Her eyes are blue, her forehead pale and meek,

Her lips like cherries on a summer tree –

Here's a health to the charming maid, who e'er she be!

When I go to the field no youth can lighter bound,

And I freely pay when the cheerful jug goes round;

The barrel is full, but its heart we soon shall see –

Come, here's to that charming maid, who e'er she be!

Had I the wealth that props the Saxon's reign,

Or the diamond crown that decks the King of Spain,

I'd yield them all if she kindly smiled on me –

Here's a health to the maid I love, who e'er she be!

Five pounds of gold for each lock of her hair I'd pay,

And five times five for my love one hour each day;

Her voice is more sweet than the thrush on its own green tree –

Then, my dear, may I drink a fond deep health to thee!

Translated by J. J. Callanan

Anonymous *(18th century)*

THE FAIR-HAIRED GIRL

The sun has set, the stars are still,

The red moon hides behind the hill;

The tide has left the brown beach bare,

The birds have fled the upper air;

Below. Traditional cottage in County Donegal

Upon her branch the lone cuckoo

Is chanting still her sad adieu;

And you, my fair-haired girl, must go

Across the salt sea under woe!

I through love have learned three things,

Sorrow, sin, and death it brings;

Yet day by day my heart within

Dares shame and sorrow, death and sin:

Maiden, you have aimed the dart

Rankling in my ruined heart:

Maiden, may the God above

Grant you grace to grant me love!

Sweeter than the viol's string,

And the notes that blackbirds sing;

Brighter than the dewdrops rare

Is the maiden wondrous fair:

Like the silver swans at play

Is her neck, as bright as day!

Woe is me, that e'er my sight

Dwelt on charms so deadly bright!

Translated by Samuel Ferguson

Anonymous (18th century)

DEAR DARK HEAD

Put your head, darling, darling, darling,

Your darling black head my heart above;

Oh, mouth of honey, with the thyme for fragrance,

Who, with heart in breast, could deny you love?

Oh, many and many a young girl for me is pining,

Letting her locks of gold to the cold wind free,

For me, the foremost of our gay young fellows;

But I'd leave a hundred, pure love, for thee!

Then put your head, darling, darling, darling,

Your darling black head my heart above;

Oh, mouth of honey, with the thyme for fragrance,

Who, with heart in breast, could deny you love?

Translated by Samuel Ferguson

Anonymous (18th century)

THE LITTLE WHITE CAT

The little gray cat was walking prettily,

When she found her little son stretched dead

And 'twas only a year since her family

Were cast out and drowned in a trench.

The little white cat, white, white, white,

The little white cat, Breed's cat.

The little white cat, snowy white

That was drowned in a trench.

The little mother stood upright,

When she found her little son dead;

She brought him in and made a bed for him,

And then began to lament him.

The little white cat, white, white, white,

The little white cat, Breed's cat.

The little white cat, snowy white

That was drowned in a trench.

Andrew, the blind, had some of her family,

And they came together to lament him,

I am sure if Barry hears it,

He will regret the death of Breed's cat.

The little white cat, white, white, etc.

He broke no chest, nor lock of the neighbours,

Nor did he destroy the cows' butter.

And you never heard such discourse,

Below. Cork Harbour, County Cork

As the mice had in telling it.

The little white cat, white, white, white,

The little white cat, Breed's cat.

That was drowned in a trench.

Extract. Translated by Mrs Costello of Tuam

Anonymous

HOW HAPPY THE LITTLE BIRDS

How happy the little birds

That rise up on high

And make music together

On a single bough!

Not so with me

And my hundred thousand loves:

Far apart on us

Rises every day.

Whiter she than the lily,

Than beauty more fair,

Sweeter voiced than the violin,

More lightsome than the sun;

Yet beyond all that

Her nobleness, her mind, –

And O God Who art in Heaven,

Relieve my pain!

Translated by Padraic Pearse

Jonathan Swift *(1667-1745)*

The two poems that follow belong to 'Verses for Fruit-women. They are to be found in Jonathan's Swift's Collected Works, first published in Dublin in 1795.

APPLES

Come buy my fine wares,

Plums, apples, and pears.

A hundred a penny,

In conscience too many:

Come, will you have any?

My children are seven,

I wish them in Heaven;

My husband a sot,

With his pipe and his pot,

Not a farthing will gain them,

And I must maintain them.

ONIONS

Come, follow me by the smell,

Here are delicate onions to sell;

I promise to use you well.

They make the blood warmer,

You'll feed like a farmer;

For this is every cook's opinion,

No savoury dish without an onion;

But, lest your kissing should be spoiled,

Your onions must be thoroughly boiled:

Or else you may spare

Your mistress a share,

The secret will never be known:

She cannot discover

The breath of her lover,

But think it as sweet as her own.

LULLABY OF THE WOMAN OF THE MOUNTAIN

O little head of gold! O candle of my house!

Thou wilt guide all who travel this country.

Be quiet, O house! And O little grey mice,

Stay at home to-night in your hidden lairs!

Below. Limerick Castle

O moths on the window, fold your wings!

Stay at home to-night, O little black chafers!

O plover and O curlew, over my house do not travel!

Speak not, O barnacle-goose, going over the mountain here!

O creatures of the mountain, that wake so early

Stir not to-night till the sun whitens over you.

Translated by Thomas MacDonagh

Anonymous Street Ballads

I KNOW WHERE I'M GOING

I know where I'm going,

I know who's going with me,

I know who I love,

But the dear knows who I'll marry.

I'll have stockings of silk,

Shoes of fine green leather,

Combs to buckle my hair

And a ring for every finger.

Feather beds are soft,

Painted rooms are bonny;

But I'd leave them all

To go with my love Johnny.

Some say he's dark,

I say he's bonny,

He's the flower of them all

My handsome, coaxing Johnny.

I know where I'm going,

I know who's going with me,

I know who I love,

But the dear knows who I'll marry

THE MAID THAT SOLD HER BARLEY

It's cold and raw the north winds blow

Black in the morning early,

When all the hills were covered with snow,

Oh when it was winter fairly,

As I was riding over the moor,

I met a farmer's daughter,

Her cherry cheeks and sloe black eyes,

They caused my heart to falter.

I bowed my bonnet very low

To let her know my meaning.

She answered with a courteous smile,

Her looks they were engaging.

"Where are you bound my pretty maid,

It's now in the morning early?"

The answer that she made to me,

"Kind Sir, to sell my barley."

"Now twenty guineas I've in my purse,

And twenty more that's yearly,

You need not go to the market town,

For I'll buy all your barley.

If twenty guineas would gain the heart,

Of the maid that I love so dearly,

All for to tarry with me one night,

And go home in the morning early."

As I was riding o'er the moor,

The very evening after,

It was my fortune for to meet

The farmer's only daughter.

Although the weather being cold and raw

With her I thought to parley,

This answer then she made to me,

"Kind sir, I've sold my barley."

Below. Kelp burning, Renvyle, Connemara

I WANT TO BE MARRIED AND CANNOT TELL HOW

To the field I carried my milking pail

On a May day morning early,

And there I met with a smart young man,

Who said that he lov'd me dearly.

I made him a curtsey, he made me a bow,

He kissed me, and promised to marry, I vow,

Oh! I wish that young fellow was with me just now,

On a May day morning early.

I try to forget him, but all in vain,

On every day morning early,

And if I never should see him again,

It will break my heart – or nearly,

I can't bear the sight of a sheep or cow

I want to be married and cannot tell how,

Oh! I wish that young fellow was with me now,

On a May day morning early.

Like him, the sprite,

Whom maids by night

Oft meet in glen that's haunted.

Like him, too, beauty won me,

But while her eyes were on me,

If once their ray

Was turned away,

Oh! winds could not outrun me.

Below. The harbour, Roundstone, County Galway

Are those follies goingl

And is my proud heart growing

Too cold or wise

For brilliant eyes

Again to set it glowing?

No – vain, alas! the endeavour

From bonds so sweet to sever; –

Poor wisdom's chance

Against a glance

Is now as weak as ever!

THE MINSTREL BOY

The minstrel boy to the war is gone,

In the ranks of death you'll find him,

His father's sword he has girded on,

And his wild harp slung behind him.

"Land of songl" said the warrior bard,

"Though all the world betrays thee,

One sword, at least, thy rights shall guard,

One faithful harp shall praise thee!"

The minstrel fell! – but the foeman's chain

Could not bring his proud soul under;

The harp he loved ne'er spoke again,

For he tore its chords asunder;

And said, "No chains shall sully thee,

Thou soul of love and bravery!

Thy songs were made for the pure and free,

They shall never sound in slavery!"

BELIEVE ME, IF ALL THOSE ENDEARING
YOUNG CHARMS

Believe me, if all those endearing young charms,

Which I gaze on so fondly to-day,

Were to change by tomorrow, and fleet in my arms,

Like fairy gifts fading awayl

Thou wouldst still be adored, as this moment thou

Let thy loveliness fade as it will,

And around the dear ruin each wish of my heart

Would entwine itself verdantly still.

It is not while beauty and youth are thine own,

And thy cheeks unprofaned by a tear,

That the fervor and faith of a soul may be known,

To which time will but make thee more dear!

Oh the heart that has truly loved never forgets,

But as truly loves on to the close,

As the sunflower turns to her god when he sets

The same look which she turned when he rose!

THE LAST ROSE OF SUMMER

'Tis the last rose of summer,

Left blooming alone;

All her lovely companions

Are faded and gone;

No flower of her kindred,

No rose bud is nigh

To reflect back her blushes,

Or give sigh for sigh!

I'll not leave thee, thou lone one!

To pine on the stem;

Since the lovely are sleeping,

Go, sleep thou with them;

Thus kindly I scatter

Thy leaves o'er the bed,

Where thy mates of the garden

Lie scentless and dead.

So soon may I follow,

When friendships decay,

And from love's shining circle

Thy gems drop away!

When true hearts lie withered,

And fond ones are flown,

Oh! who would inhabit

This bleak world alone?

Below. Ballynahinch Castle, Connemara

LOVE IS A HUNTER BOY

Love is a hunter boy,

Who makes young hearts his prey

And, in his nets of joy,

Ensnares them night and day.

In vain concealed they lie –

Love tracks them everywhere;

In vain aloft they fly –

Love shoots them flying there.

But 'tis his joy most sweet,

At early dawn to trace

The print of Beauty's feet,

And give the trembler chase.

And if, through virgin snow,

He tracks her footsteps fair,

How sweet for Love to know

None went before him there.

THE SONG OF FIONNUALA

Silent, O Moyle! be the roar of thy water,

Break not, ye breezes, your chain of repose,

While, murmuring mournfully, Lir's lonely daughter

Tells to the night-star her tale of woes.

When shall the swan, her death-note singing,

Sleep, with wings in darkness furled?

When will heaven, its sweet bell ringing,

Call my spirit from this stormy world?

Sadly, O Moyle! to thy winter wave weeping,

Fate bids me languish long ages away!

Yet still in her darkness doth Erin lie sleeping,

Still doth the pure light its dawning delay!

When will that day-star, mildly springing,

Warm our isle with peace and love?

When will heaven, its sweet bell ringing,

Call my spirit to the fields above?

THE HARP THAT ONCE THROUGH TARA'S HALLS

The harp that once through Tara's halls

The soul of music shed,

Now hangs as mute on Tara's walls

As if that soul were fled.

So sleeps the pride of former days,

So glory's thrill is o'er,

And hearts that once beat high for praise,

Now feel that pulse no more!

No more to chiefs and ladies bright

The harp of Tara swells;

The chord alone that breaks at night,

Its tale of ruin tells.

Thus Freedom now so seldom wakes,

The only throb she gives

Is when some heart indignant breaks,

To show that still she lives.

James Kenney *(1780 – 1849)*

THE OLD STORY OVER AGAIN

When I was a maid,

Nor of lovers afraid,

My mother cried, "Girl, never listen to men."

Her lectures were long,

But I thought her quite wrong,

And I said, "Mother, whom should I listen to, then?"

Below. Bantry Bay

Now teaching, in turn,

What I never could learn,

I find, like my mother, my lessons all vain;

Men ever deceive, –

Silly maidens believe,

And still 'tis the old story over again.

So humbly they woo,

What can poor maidens do

But keep them alive when they swear they must die7

Ah! who can forbear,

As they weep in despair,

The crocodile tears in compassion to dry?

Yet, wedded at last,

When the honeymoon's past,

The lovers forsake us, the husbands remain;

Our vanity's checked,

And we ne'er can expect

They will tell us the old story over again.

John Anster *(1789-1867)* – two poems

IF I MIGHT CHOOSE

If I might choose where my tired limbs shall lie

When my task here is done, the oak's green crest

Shall rise above my grave – a little mound,

Raised in some cheerful village cemetery.

And I could wish, that, with unceasing sound,

A lonely mountain rill was murmuring by –

In music – through the long soft twilight hours.

And let the hand of her, whom I love best,

Plant round the bright green grave those fragrant

In whose deep bells the wild-bee loves to rest;

And should the robin from some neighboring tree

Pour his enchanted song– oh! softly tread,

For sure, if aught of earth can soothe the dead,

He still must love that pensive melody!

J. J. Callanan *(1795-1828)* – two poems

SONG

Awake thee, my Bessy, the morning is fair,

The breath of young roses is fresh on the air,

The sun has long glanced over mountain and lake –

Then awake from thy slumbers, my Bessy, awake.

Oh, come whilst the flowers are still wet with the dew –

I'll gather the fairest, my Bessy, for you;

The lark poureth forth his sweet strain for thy sake –

Then awake from thy slumbers, my Bessy, awake.

The hare from her soft bed of heather hath gone,

The coot to the water already hath flown;

There is life on the mountain and joy on the lake –

Then awake from thy slumbers, my Bessy, awake.

Opposite. The Rock of Cashel, Tipperary

SERENADE

The blue waves are sleeping;

The breezes are still;

The light dews are weeping

Soft tears on the hill;

The moon in mild beauty

Looks bright from above;

Then come to the casement,

O Mary, my love.

Not a sound or a motion

Is over the lake,

But the whisper of ripples,

As shoreward they break;

My skiff wakes no ruffle

The waters among;

Then listen, dear maid,

To thy true lover's song.

No form from the lattice

Did ever recline

Over Italy's waters,

More lovely than thine;

Then come to thy window,

And shed from above

One glance of thy dark eye,

One smile of thy love.

Oh! the soul of that eye,

When it breaks from its shroud,

Shines beauteously out,

Like the moon from a cloud;

And thy whisper of love,

Breathed thus from afar,

Is sweeter to me

Than the sweetest guitar.

From the storms of this world

How gladly I'd fly

To the calm of that breast,

To the heaven of that eye!

How deeply I love thee

'Twere useless to tell;

Farewell, then, my dear one –

My Mary, farewell.

George Darley *(1795 – 1846)* – four poems

THE SEA RITUAL

Prayer unsaid, and mass unsung,

Deadman's dirge must still be rung:

Dingle-dong, the dead-bells sound!

Mermen chant his dirge around!

Wash him bloodless, smooth his fair,

Stretch his limbs, and sleek his hair:

Dingle-dong, the dead-bells go!

Mermen swing them to and fro!

In the wormless sand shall he

Feast for no foul glutton be:

Dingle-dong, the dead-bells chime!

Mermen keep the tone and time!

We must with a tombstone brave

Shut the shark out from his grave:

Dingle-dong, the dead-bells toll!

Mermen dirgers ring his knoll!

Such a slab will we lay o'er him

All the dead shall rise before him!

Dingle-dong, the dead-bells boom!

Mermen lay him in his tomb!

Above. The Dargle, County Wicklow

SONG

Down the dimpled green-sward dancing

Bursts a flaxen headed bevy,

Bud-lipped boys and girls advancing

Love's irregular little levy.

Rows of liquid eyes in laughter, –

How they glimmer, how they quiver!

Sparkling one another after,

Like the ripples on a river.

Tipsy band of rubious faces,

Flushed with joys ethereal spirit,

Make your mocks and sly grimaces

At Love's self, and do not fear it.

ROBIN'S CROSS

A little cross,

To tell my loss;

A little bed

To rest my head;

A little tear is all I crave

Under my very little grave.

I strew thy bed

Who loved thy lays

The tear I shed,

The cross I raise,

With nothing more upon it than –

Here lies the little Friend of Man

LAST NIGHT

I sat with one I love last night,

She sang to me an olden strain;

In former times it woke delight,

Last night – but pain.

Last night we saw the stars arise,

But clouds soon dimmed the ether blue;

And when we sought each other's eyes

Tears dimmed them too!

We paced along our favorite walk,

But paced in silence broken-hearted:

Of old we used to smile and talk;

Last night – we parted.

❦❦

Samuel Lover *(1797-1868)* – two poems

WHAT WILL YOU DO, LOVE?

"What will you do, love, when I am going,

With white sail flowing,

The seas beyond? –

What will you do, love, when waves divide us,

And friends may chide us

For being fond?"

"Though waves divide us, and friends be chiding,

In faith abiding,

I'll still be true!l

And I'll pray for thee on the stormy ocean,

In deep devotion –

That's what I'll do!"

"What would you do, love. if distant tidings

Thy fond confidings

Should undermine? –

And I, abiding 'neath sultry skies,

Should think other eyes

Were as bright as thine?"

"Oh, name it not! – though guilt and shame

Were on thy name,

I'd still be true:

But that heart of thine – should another share it –

could not bear it!

What would I do?"

Below. The road to Dugort, Achill Island

"What would you do, love, when home returning,

With hopes high-burning,

With wealth for you,

If my bark, which bounded o'er foreign foam,

Should be lost near home –

Ah! what would you do?"

"So thou wert spared – I'd bless the morrow

In want and sorrow,

That left me you

And I'd welcome thee from the wasting billow,

This heart thy pillow –

That's what I'd do!"

THE ANGEL'S WHISPER

A superstition of great beauty prevails in Ireland, that when a child smiles
in its sleep, it is "talking with angels."

A baby was sleeping,

Its mother was weeping,

For her husband was far on the wild raging sea;

And the tempest was swelling

Round the fisherman's dwelling,

And she cried, "Dermot, darling, oh! come back to me."

Her beads while she number'd,

The baby still slumber'd,

And smiled in her face as she bended her knee;

"Oh blest be that warning,

My child's sleep adorning,

For I know that the angels are whispering with thee.

"And while they are keeping

Bright watch o'er thy sleeping,

Oh, pray to them softly, my baby, with me

And say thou wouldst rather

They'd watch o'er thy father! –

For I know that the angels are whispering with thee."

The dawn of the morning

Saw Dermot returning,

And the wife wept with joy her babe's father to see;

And closely caressing

Her child, with a blessing,

Said, "I knew that the angels were whispering with thee."

Gerald Griffin *(1803 – 1840)* – two poems

I LOVE MY LOVE IN THE MORNING

love my love in the morning,

For she like morn is fair –

Her blushing cheek, its crimson streak,

It clouds her golden hair.

Her glance, its beam, so soft and kind;

Her tears, its dewy showers;

And her voice, the tender whispering win~

That stirs the early bowers.

I love my love in the morning,

I love my love at noon,

For she is bright as the lord of light,

Yet mild as autumn's moon:

Her beauty is my bosom's sun,

Her faith my fostering shade,

And I will love my darling one,

Till even the sun shall fade.

I love my love in the morning,

I love my love at even;

Her smile's soft play is like the ray

That lights the western heaven:

I loved her when the sun was high,

I loved her when he rose;

But best of all when evening's sigh

Was murmuring at its close.

Below. Maggillicuddy's Rocks, Killarney

GONE! GONE! FOREVER GONE

Gone, gone, forever gone

Are the hopes I cherished,

Changed like the sunny dawn,

In sudden showers perished.

Withered is the early flower,

Like a bright lake brolten,

Faded like a happy hour,

Or Love's secret spoken.

Life! what a cheat art thou!

On youthful fancy stealing,

A prodigal in promise now;

A miser in fulfilling!

Thomas Osborne Davis *(1814 – 1845)* two poems

MY GRAVE

Shall they bury me in the deep,

Where wind-forgetting waters sleep?

Where wind-forgetting waters sleep?

Shall they dig a grave for me,

Under the green-wood tree7

Or on the wild heath,

Where the wilder breath

Of the storm doth blow?

Oh, no! oh, no!

Shall they bury me in the Palace Tombs,

Or under the shade of Cathedral domes?

Sweet 't were to lie on Italy's shore;

Yet not there – nor in Greece, though I love it more.

In the wolf or the vulture my grave shall I find?

Shall my ashes career on the world-seeing wind?

Shall they fling my corpse in the battle mound,

Where coffinless thousands lie under the ground?

Just as they fall they are buried so –

Oh, no! oh, no!

No! on an Irish green hill-side,

On an opening lawn – but not too wide;

For I love the drip of the wetted trees –

I love not the gales, but a gentle breeze,

To freshen the turf – put no tombstone there,

But green sods decked with daisies fair;

Nor sods too deep, but so that the dew,

The matted grass-roots may trickle through.

Be my epitaph writ on my country's mind,

"He served his country, and loved his kind."

Oh! 't were merry unto the grave to go,

If one were sure to be buried so.

THE GIRL I LEFT BEHIND ME

The dames of France are fond and free,

And Flemish lips are willing,

And soft the maids of Italy,

And Spanish eyes are thrilling;

Still, though I bask beneath their smile,

Their charms fail to bind me,

And my heart flies back to Erin's isle,

To the girl I left behind me.

For she's as fair as Shannon's side,

And purer than its water,

But she refused to be my bride

Though many a year I sought her;

Yet, since to France I sailed away,

Her letters oft remind me

That I promised never to gainsay

The girl I left behind me.

She says – "My own dear love, come home,

My friends are rich and many,

Below. A garden at Leenane, Connemara

Or else abroad with you I'll roam

A soldier stout as any;

If you'll not come, nor let me go,

I'll think you have resigned me."

My heart nigh broke when I answered – No!

To the girl I left behind me.

For never shall my true love brave

A life of war and toiling;

And never as a skulking slave

I'll tread my native soil on;

But, were it free, or to be freed,

The battle's close would find me

To Ireland bound – nor message need

From the girl I left behind me.

William Pembroke Mulchinock *(1820?–1864)*

THE ROSE OF TRALEE

The pale moon was rising above the green mountain,

The sun was declining beneath the blue sea,

When I stray'd with my love to the pure crystal fountain

That stands in the beautiful vale of Tralee.

She was lovely and fair as the rose of the summer,

Yet 'twas not her beauty alone that won me,

Oh, no, 'twas the truth in her eyes ever beaming

That made me love Mary, the Rose of Tralee.

The cool shades of evening their mantle were spreading,

And Mary, all smiling, was list'ning to me,

The moon through the valley her pale rays was shedding

When I won the heart of the Rose of Tralee.

Tho' lovely and fair as the rose of the summer,

Yet 'twas not her beauty alone that won me,

Oh, no, 'twas the truth in her eyes ever beaming

That made me love Mary, the Rose of Tralee.

Cecil Frances Alexander *(1820? – 1895)*

DREAMS

Beyond, beyond the mountain line,

The grey-stone and the boulder,

Beyond the growth of dark green pine,

That crowns its western shoulder,

There lies that fairy-land of mine,

Unseen of a beholder.

Its fruits are all like rubies rare;

Its streams are clear as glasses;

There golden castles hang in air,

And purple grapes in masses,

And noble knights and ladies fair

Come riding down the passes.

Ah me! they say if I could stand

Upon those mountain ledges,

I should but see on either hand

Plain fields and dusty hedges;

And yet I know my fairy-land

Lies somewhere o'er their edges.

Richard D'Alton Williams *(1822–1862)* – extract

THE DYING GIRL

From a Munster vale they brought her,

From the pure and balmy air;

An Ormond peasant's daughter,

With blue eyes and golden hair.

They brought her to the city

And she faded slowly there –

Consumption has no pity

For blue eyes and golden hair.

Below. A cottage interior, Achill Island

When I saw her first reclining

Her lips were mov'd in prayer,

And the setting sun was shining

On her loosen'd golden hair.

When our kindly glances met her,

Deadly brilliant was her eye;

And she said that she was better,

While we knew that she must die.

She speaks of Munster valleys,

The pattern, dance, and fair,

And her thin hand feebly dallies

With her scattered golden hair.

When silently we listen'd

To her breath with quiet care,

Her eyes with wonder glisten'd,

And she asked us, "What was there?"

The poor thing smiled to ask it,

And her pretty mouth laid bare,

Like gems within a casket,

A string of pearlets rare.

We said that we were trying

By the gushing of her blood

And the time she took in sighing

To know if she were good.

Well, she smil'd and chatted gaily,

Though we saw in mute despair

The hectic brighter daily,

And the death-dew on her hair.

And oft her wasted fingers

Beating time upon the bed:

O'er some old tune she lingers,

And she bows her golden head.

Before the sun had risen

Through the lark-loved morning air,

Her young soul left its prison,

Undefiled by sin or care.

I stood beside the couch in tears

Where pale and calm she slept,

And though I've gazed on death for years,

I blush not that I wept.

I check'd with effort pity's sighs

And left the matron there,

To close the curtains of her eyes

And bind her golden hair.

Stopford A. Brooke *(1832– 1916)*

THE EARTH AND MAN

A little sun, a little rain,

A soft wind blowing from the west,

And woods and fields are sweet again,

And warmth within the mountain's breast.

So simple is the earth we tread,

So quick with love and life her frame,

Ten thousand years have dawned and fled,

And still her magic is the same.

A little love, a little trust,

A soft impulse, a sudden dream,

And life as dry as desert dust

Is fresher than a mountain stream.

So simple is the heart of man,

So ready for new hope and joy;

Ten thousand years since it began

Have left it younger than a boy.!

George Sigerson *(1835 – 1925)*

BANTRY BAY

As I'm sitting all alone in the gloaming,

It might have been but yesterday, That I watched the fisher sails all homing,

Till the little herring fleet at anchor lay;

Below. Glendalough

Then the fisher girls with baskets swinging,

Came running down the old stone way,

Every lassie to her sailor lad was singing

A welcome back to Bantry Bay.

Then we heard the piper's sweet note tuning,

And all the lassies turned to hear,

Till it mingled with a soft voice crooning,

Till the music floated down the wooden pier;

"Save ye kindly, colleens all" – said the piper,

"Hands across and trip it while I play." –

And a tender sound of song and merry dancing,

Stole softly over Bantry Bay.

As I'm sitting all alone in the gloaming,

The shadows of the past draw near,

And I see the loving faces round me,

That used to glad the old brown pier;

Some are gone upon their last long homing,

Some are left, but they are old and grey,

And we're waiting for the tide in the gloaming

To sail upon the Great Highway,

To the Land of Rest Unending –

All peacefully from Bantry Bay.

Arthur O'Shaughnessy *(1844 – 1881)* – two poems

ODE

We are the music-makers,

And we are the dreamers of dreams,

Wandering by lone sea-breakers,

And sitting by desolate streams; –

World-losers and world-forsakers,

On whom the pale moon gleams:

Yet we are the movers and shakers

Of the world for ever, it seems.

With wonderful deathless ditties

We build up the world's great cities,

And out of a fabulous story

We fashion an empire's glory:

One man with a dream, at pleasure,

Shall go forth and conquer a crown;

And three with a new song's measure

Can trample an empire down.

We, in the ages lying

In the buried past of the earth,

Built Nineveh with our sighing,

And Babel itself with our mirth:

And o'erthrew them with prophesying

To the old of the new world's worth;

For each age is a dream that is dying,

Or one that is coming to birth.

THE LINE OF BEAUTY

When mountains crumble and rivers all run dry,

When every flower has fallen and summer fails

To come again, when the sun's splendour pales,

And earth with lagging footsteps seems well-nigh

Spent in her annual circuit through the sky;

When love is a quenched flame, and nought avails

To save decrepit man, who feebly wails

And lies down lost in the great grave to die;

What is eternal? What escapes decay?

A certain faultless, matchless, deathless line,

Curving consummate. Death, Eternity,

And nought to it, from it take nought away:

Twas all God's gift and all man's mastery,

God become human and man grown divine.

William Allingham *(1824 – 1889)* – two poems

THE EVICTION

In early morning twilight, raw and chill,

Damp vapours brooding on the barren hill,

Through miles of mire in steady grave array

Threescore well-arm'd police pursue their way;

Below. The Erriff Valley, County Galway

Each tall and bearded man a rifle swings,

And under each greatcoat a bayonet clings;

The Sheriff on his sturdy cob astride

Talks with the chief, who marches by their side,

And, creeping on behind them, Paudeen Dhu

Pretends his needful duty much to rue.

Six big-boned labourers, clad in common frieze,

Walk in the midst, the Sheriff's staunch allies;

Six crowbar men, from distant county brought, –

Orange, and glorying in their work, 'tis thought,

But wrongly, – churls of Catholics are they,

And merely hired at half-a-crown a day.

The Hamlet clustering on its hill is seen,

A score of petty homesteads, dark and mean;

poor always, not despairing until now;

Long used, as well as poverty knows how,

With life's oppressive trifles to contend.

This day will bring its history to an end.

Moveless and grim against the cottage walls

Lean a few silent men: but someone calls

Far off; and then a child 'without a stitch'

Runs out of doors, flies back with piercing screech,

And soon from house to house is heard the cry

Of female sorrow, swelling loud and high,

Which makes the men blaspheme between their teeth,

Meanwhile, o'er fence and watery field beneath,

The little army moves through drizzling rain;

A 'Crowbar' leads the Sheriff's nag; the lane

Is enter'd, and their plashing tramp draws near:

One instant, outcry holds its breath to hear;

'Halt!' – at the doors they form in double line,

And ranks of polish'd rifles wetly shine.

The Sheriff's painful duty must be done;

He begs for quiet – and the work's begun.

The strong stand ready; now appear the rest,

Girl, matron, Grandsire, baby on the breast,

And Rosy's thin face on a pallet borne;

A motley concourse, feeble and forlorn.

One old man, tears upon his wrinkled cheek,

Stands trembling on a threshold, tries to speak,

But, in defect of any word for this,

Mutely upon the doorpost prints akiss,

Then passes out for ever. Through the crowd

The children run bewilder'd, wailing loud;

Where needed most, the men combine their aid;

And, last of all, is Oona forth convey'd,

Reclined in her accustom'd strawen chair,

Her aged eyelids closed, her thick white hair

Escaping from her cap; she feels the chill,

Looks round and murmurs, then again is still.

Now bring the remnants of each household fire.

On the the wet grounds the hissing coals expire;

And Paudeen Dhu, with meekly dismal face,

Receives the full possession of the place.

Wherepon the Sheriff, 'We have legal hold.

Return to shelter with the sick and old.

Time shall be given; and there are carts below

If any to the workhouse choose to go.'

A young man makes him answer, grave and clear,

'We're thankful to you! but there's no one here

Goin' back intothem houses: do your part.

Nor we won't trouble Pigot's horse and cart.'

At which name, rushing into th' open space,

A woman flings her hood from off her face,

Falls on her knees upon the miry ground,

Lifts hands and eyes, and voice of thrilling sound, –

'Vengeance of God Almighty fall on you,

James Pigot! – may the poor man's curse pursue,

The widow's and the orphan's curse, I pray,

Hang heavy round you at your dying day!'

Breathless and fix'd one moment stands the crowd

To hear this malediction fierce and loud.

But now (our neighbour Neal is busy there)

On steady poles he lifted Oona's chair,

Below. The Sea Caves of Ballybunnion, County Kerry

Well-heap'd with borro'd mantles; gently bear

The sick girl in her litter, bed and all;

Whilst others hug the children weak and small

In careful arms, or hoist them pick-a-back;

And, 'midst the unrelenting clink and thwack

Of iron bar on stone, let creep away

the sad procession from that hill-side grey,

Through the slow-falling rain. In three hours more

You find, where Ballytullagh stood before,

Mere shatter'd walls, and doors with useless latch,

And firesides buried under fallen thatch.

THE DREAM

I heard the dogs howl in the moonlight night;

I went to the window to see the sight;

All the Dead that ever I knew

Going one by one and two by two.

On they pass'd, and on they pass'd;

Townsfellows all, from first to last;

Born in the moonlight of the lane,

Quenched in the heavy shadow again.

Schoolmates, marching as when we play'd
At soldiers once – but now more staid;
Those were the strangest sight to me
Who were drown'd, I knew, in the awful sea.

Straight and handsome folk; bent and weak too;
Some that I loved, and gasp'd to speak to;
Some but a day in their churchyard bed;
some that I had not known were dead ...

On, on a moving bridge they made
Across the moon-streams, from shad to shade,
Young and old, women and men;
Many long forgot, but remember'd then.

And first there came a bitter laughter;
A sound of tears the moment after;
And then a music so lofty and gay,
That every morning, day by day,
I strive to recall it if I may.

John Boyle O'Reilly *(1844 – 1890)* – seven poems

THE CRY OF THE DREAMER

I am tired of planning and toiling

In the crowded hives of men;

Heart-weary of building and spoiling

And spoiling and building again.

And I long for the dear old river,

Where I dreamed my youth away

For a dreamer lives forever,

And a toiler dies in a day

I am sick of the showy seeming

Of a life that is half a lie;

Of the faces lined with scheming

In the throng that hurries by.

From the sleepless thoughts' endeavour,

I would go where the children play;

For a dreamer lives forever,

And a thinker dies in a day.

I can feel no pride but pity

For the burdens the rich endure;

There is nothing sweet in the city

But the patient lives of the poor.

Ah, the little hands too skillful,

And the child-mind choked with weeds!

The daughter's heart grown willful,

And the father's heart that bleeds!

Below. The Claddagh, County Galway

No!, No! from the street's rude bustle,

From trophies of mart and stage,

I would fly to the woods'' low rustle

And the meadows' kindly page.

Let me dream as of old by the river,

And be loved for the dream always;

For a dreamer lives forever,

And a toiler dies in a day.

DISAPPOINTMENT

Her hair was a waving bronze and her eyes

Deep wells that might cover a brooding soul;

And who, till he weighed it, could ever surmise

That her heart was a cinder instead of a coal?

CONSTANCY

"You gave me the key of your heart, my love;

Then why do you make me knock?"

"Oh, that was yesterday, Saints above!

And last night – I changed the lock!"

A WHITE ROSE

The red rose whispers of passion,

And the white rose breathes of love;

Oh, the red rose. is a falcon,

And the white rose is a dove.

Below. The Upper Lake, Killarney

But I send you a cream-white rosebud

With a flush on its petal tips;

For the love that is purest and sweetest

Has a kiss of desire on the lips.

TO-DAY

Only from day to day

The life of a wise man runs;

What matter if seasons far away

Have gloom or have double suns?

To climb the unreal path,

We stray from the roadway here;

We swim the rivers of wrath

And tunnel the hills of fear.

Our feet on the torrent's brink,

Our eyes on the cloud afar,

We fear the things we think,

Instead of the things that are.

Like a tide our work should rise,

Each later wave the best;

"To-day is a king in disguise,"

To-day is the special test.

Like a sawyer's work is life –

The present makes the flaw,

And the only field for strife

Is the inch before the saw

THE INFINITE

The infinite always is silent:

It is only the Finite speaks.

Our words are the idle wave-caps

On the deep that never breaks.

We may question with wand of science,

Explain, decide and discuss;

But only in meditation

The Mystery speaks to us.

FOREVER

Those we love truly never die,

Though year by year the sad memorial wreath,

A ring and flowers, types of life and death,

Are laid upon their graves.

For death the pure life saves,

And life all pure is love; and love can reach

From heaven to earth, and nobler lessons teach

than those by mortals read.

Well blest is he who has a dear one dead:

A friend he has whose face will never change –

A dear communion that will not grow strange:

The anchor of a love is death.

The blessed sweetness of a loving breath

Will reach our cheek all fresh through weary years

For her who died long since, ah! waste not tears,

She's thine unto the end.

Thank God for one dear friend,

With face still radiant with the light of truth,

Whose love comes laden with scent of youth,

Through twenty years of death.

Oscar Wilde *(1854 – 1900)*

REQUIESCAT

Thread lightly, she is near

Under the snow,

Speak gently, she can hear

The daisies grow.

Below. Menaun Cliffs, Achill Island

All her bright golden hair

Tarnished with rust,

She that was young and fair

Fallen to dust.

Lily-like, white as snow,

She hardly knew

She was a woman, so

Sweetly she grew.

Coffin-board, heavy stone,

Lie on her breast,

I vex my heart alone,

She is at rest.

Peace, Peace, she cannot hear

Lyre or sonnet,

All my life's buried here,

Heap earth upon it.

Aubrey de Vere *(1814– 1902)*

HUMAN LIFE

Sad is our youth, for it is ever going,

Crumbling away beneath our very feet;

Sad is our life, for onward it is flowing,

In current unperceived because so fleet;

Sad are our hopes, for they were sweet in sowing

But tares, self-sown, have overtopped the wheat;

Sad are our joys, for they were sweet in blowing;

And still, O still, their dying breath is sweet:

And sweet is youth, although it hath bereft us

Of that which made our childhood sweeter still:

And sweet our life's decline, for it hath left us

A nearer Good to cure an older ill:

And sweet are all things, when we learn to prize them

Not for their sake, but His who grants them or denies them.

William Edward Hartpole Lecky *(1838 – 1903)*

EARLY THOUGHTS

Oh gather the thoughts of your early years,

Gather them as they flow,

For all unmarked in those thoughts appears

The path where you soon must go.

Full many a dream will wither away,

And Springtide hues are brief,

But the lines are there of the autumn day,

Like the skeleton in the leaf.

The husbandman knows not the worth of his seed

Until the flower be sprung,

And only in age can we rightly read

The thoughts that we thought when young.

Ethna Carbery *(1866 – 1902)*

THE LOVE-TALKER

I met the Love-Talker one eve in the glen,

He was handsomer than any of our handsome young men

Below. Reflections, Kylemore Lough

His eyes were blacker than the sloe, his voice sweeter far

Than the crooning of old Kevin's pipes beyond in Coolnagar.

I was bound for the milking with a heart fair and free –

My grief! my grief! that bitter hour drained the life from me;

I thought him human lover, though his lips on mine were cold,

And the breath of death blew keen on me within his hold.

I know not what way he came, no shadow fell behind,

But all the sighing rushes swayed beneath a fairy wind;

The thrush ceased its singing, a mist crept about,

We two clung together – with the world shut out.

Beyond the ghostly mist I could hear my cattle low,

The little cow from Ballina, clean as driven snow,

The dun cow from Kerry, the roan from Inisheer,

Oh, pitiful their calling – and his whispers in my ear!

His eyes were a fire; his words were a snare;

I cried my mother's name, but no help was there;

I made the blessed Sign – then he gave a dreary moan,

A wisp of cloud went floating by, and I stood alone.

Running ever thro' my head is an old-time rune –

"Who meets the Love-Talker must weave her shroud soon."

My mother's face is furrowed with the salt tears that fall,

But the kind eyes of my father are the saddest sight of all.

I have spun the fleecy lint and now my wheel is still,

The linen length is woven for my shroud fine and chill,

I shall stretch me on the bed where a happy maid I lay –

Pray for the soul of Maire Og at dawning of the day!

Edward Dowden *(1843 – 1913)*

AUTUMN SONG

Long Autumn rain;

White mists which choke the vale, and blot the sides

Of the bewildered hills; in all the plain

No field agleam where the gold pageant was,

And silent o'er a tangle of drenched grass

The blackbird glides.

In the heart, – fire,

Fire and clear air and cries of water-springs,

And large, pure winds; all April's quick desire,

All June's possession; a most fearless Earth

Drinking great ardours; and the rapturous birth

Of winged things.

Emily Lawless *(1845 – 1913)*

THE STRANGER'S GRAVE

Little feet too young and soft to walk,

Little lips too young and pure to talk,

Little faded grass-tufts, root and stalk.

I lie alone here, utterly alone,

Amid pure ashes my wild ashes mingle;

A drowned man, with a name, unknown,

A drifting waif, flung by the drifting shingle.

Oh, plotting brain, and restless heart of mine,

What strange fate brought you to so strange a shrine?

Sometimes a woman comes across the grass,

Bare-footed, with pit-patterings scarcely heard,

Sometimes the grazing cattle slowly pass,

Or on my turf sings loud some mating bird.

Oh, plotting brain, and restless heart of mine,

What strange fate brought you to so strange a shrine?

Little feet too young and soft to walk,

Little lips too young and pure to talk,

Little faded grass-tufts, root and stalk.

Below. The ancient walled city of Athenry, County Galway

Padraic Pearse *(1879 – 1916)* – two poems

Padraic Pearse took part in the 1916 Easter Uprising and was executed in that same year. He wrote this poem at his mother's request, before he and his brother departed to join the insurrection.

THE MOTHER

I do not grudge them; Lord, I do not grudge

My two strong sons that I have seen go out

To break their strength and die, they and a few,

In bloody protest for a glorious thing.

They shall be spoken of among their people,

The generations shall remember them,

And call them blessed;

But I will speak their names to my own heart

In the long nights;

The little names that were familiar once

Round my dead hearth.

Lord, thou art hard on mothers:

We suffer in their coming and their going;

And tho' I grudge them not, I weary, weary

Of the long sorrow—And yet I have my joy:

My sons were faithfuL and they fought.

IDEAL

Naked I saw thee,

O beauty of beauty!

And I blinded my eyes

For fear I should flinch.

I heard thy music,

O sweetness of sweetness!

And I shut my ears

For fear I should fail.

I kissed thy lips

O sweetness of sweetness!

And I hardened my heart

For fear of my ruin.

I blinded my eyes

And my ears I shut,

I hardened my heart,

And my love I quenched.

I turned my back

On the dream I had shaped,

And to this road before me

My face I turned.

I set my face

To the road here before me,

To the work that I see,

To the death that I shall meet.

Thomas MacDonagh *(1878 – 1916 – two poems*

IN PARIS

So here is my desert and here am I

In the midst of it alone,

Silent and free as a hawk in the sky,

Unnoticed and unknown.

I speak to no one from sun to sun,

And do my single will,

Though round me loud voiced millions run

And life is never still.

There goes the bell of the Sorbonne

Just as in Villon's day –

He heard it here go sounding on,

And stopped his work to pray –

Just in this place, in time of snow,

Alone, at a table bent –

Four hundred and fifty years ago

He wrote that Testament.

Below. Carlingford Lough, County Down

THE MAN UPRIGHT

I once spent an evening in a village

Where the people are all taken up with tillage,

Or do some business in a small way

Among themselves, and all the day

Go crooked, doubled to half their size,

Both by working and loafing, with their eyes

Stuck in the ground or in a board, –

For some of them tailor, and some of them hoard

Pence in a till in their little shops,

And some of them shoe-soles – they get the tops

Ready-made from England, and they die cobblers –

All bent up double, a village of hobblers

And slouchers and squatters, whether they straggle

Up and down, or bend to haggle

Over a counter, or bend at a plough,

Or to dig with a spade, or to milk a cow

Or to shove the goose-iron stiffly along

The stuff on the sleeve-board, or lace the fong

In the boot on the last, or to draw the wax-end

Tight cross-ways – and so to make or to mend

What will soon be worn out by the crooked people,

The only thing straight in the place was the steeple,

I thought at first. it was wrong in that;

For there past the window at which I sat

Watching the crooked little men

Go slouching, and with the gait of a hen

An odd little woman go pattering past,

And the cobbler crouching over his last

In his window opposite, and next door

The tailor squatting inside on the floor –

While I watched them, as I have said before,

And thought that only the steeple was straight,

There came a man of a different gait –

A man who neither slouched nor pattered,

But planted his steps as if each step mattered,

Yet walked down the middle of the street

Not like a policeman on his beat,

But like a man with nothing to do

Except walk straight upright like me and you.

Francis Ledwidge *(1891 – 1917)* – two poems

THE HERONS

As I was climbing Ardan Mor

From the shore of Sheelin lake,

I met the herons coming down

Before the water's wake.

And they were talking in their flight

Of dreamy ways the herons go

When all the hills are withered up

Nor any waters flow

A LITTLE BOY IN THE MORNING

He will not come, and still I wait.

He whistles at another gate

Where angels listen. Ah, I know

He will not come, yet if I go

How shall I know he did not pass

Barefooted in the flowery grass?

The moon leans on one silver horn

Above the silhouettes of morn,

And from their nest sills finches whistle

Or stooping pluck the downy thistle.

How is the morn so gay and fair

Without his whistling in its air?

The world is calling, I must go.

How shall I know he did not pass

Barefooted in the shining grass?

Thomas M. Kettle *(1880 - 1916)*

TO MY DAUGHTER BETTY, THE GIFT OF GOD

In wiser days, my darling rosebud, blown

To beauty proud as was your mother's prime,

In that desired, delayed, incredible time,

You'll ask why I abandoned you, my own,

Below. The Rosses, County Donnegal

And the dear heart that was your baby throne,

To dice with death. And oh! they'll give you rhyme

And reason: some will call the thing sublime,

And some decry it in a knowing tone.

So here, while the mad guns curse overhead,

And tired men sigh with mud for couch and floor,

Know that we fools, now with the foolish dead,

Died not for flag, nor King, nor Emperor –

But for a dream, born in a herdman's shed,

And for the secret Scripture of the poor.

Dora Sigerson Shorter *(1866 – 1917)*

THE PIPER ON THE HILL (A Child's Song)

There sits a piper on the hill

Who pipes the livelong day,

And when he pipes both loud and shrill,

The frightened people say:

"The wind, the wind is blowing up

'Tis rising to a gale,"

The women hurry to the shore

To watch some distant sail.

The wind, the wind, the wind, the wind

Is blowing to a gale.

But when he pipes all sweet and low,

The piper on the hill,

I hear the merry women go

With laughter, loud and shrill:

"The wind, the wind is coming south

'Twill blow a gentle day."

They gather on the meadow-land

To toss the yellow hay.

The wind, the wind, the wind, the wind

Is blowing blowing south to-day.

And in the morn, when winter comes,

To keep the piper warm,

The little Angels shake their wings

To make a feather storm:

"the snow, the snow has come at last!"

The happy children call.

And "ring around" they dance in glee,

And watch the nowflakes fall.

Has spread a snowy pall.

But when at night the piper plays,

I have no any fear,

Because God's windows open wide

The pretty tune to hear;

And when each crowding spirit looks,

From its star's window-pane,

A watching mother may behold

Her little child again.

The wind, the wind, the wind, the wind

May blow her home again.

Emily Henrietta Hickey *(1845 – 1924)*

BELOVED, IT IS MORN!

Beloved, it is morn!

A redder berry on the thorn,

A deeper yellow on the corn,

For this good day new-born.

Pray, Sweet, for me

That I may be

Faithful to God and thee.

Beloved, it is day!

And lovers work, as children play,

With heart and brain untired alway:

Dear love, look up and pray.

Pray, Sweet, for me

That I may be

Faithful to God and thee.

Below. Lakes of Killarney from Kenmare road

Beloved, it is night!

Thy heart and mine are full of light,

Thy spirit shineth clear and white,

God keep thee in His sight!

Pray, Sweet, for me

That I may be

Faithful to God and thee.

❧❧

Thomas Boyd *(1867 – 1927)*

THE HEATH

Through the purple dusk on this pathless heath

Wanders a horse with its rider, Death.

The steed like its master is old and grim,

And the flame in his eye is burning dim.

The crown of the rider is red with gold,

For he is lord of the lea and the wold.

A-tween his ribs, against the sky

Glimmer the stars as he rideth by.

A hungry scythe o'er his shoulder bare

Glints afar through the darkening air,

And the sudden clank of his horse's hoof

Frightens the Wanderer aloof.

Eva Gore-Booth *(1870 – 1926)*

THE LITTLE WAVES OF BREFFNY

The grand road from the mountain goes shining to the sea,

And there is traffic in it and many a horse and cart,

But the little roads of Cloonagh are dearer far to me,

And the little roads of Cloonagh go rambling through my heart.

A great storm from the ocean goes shouting o'er the hill,

And there is glory in it and terror on the wind,

But the haunted air of twilight is very strange and still,

And the little winds of twilight are dearer to my mind.

The great waves of the Atlantic sweep storming on the way,

Shining green and silver with the hidden herring shoal,

But the Little Waves of Breffny have drenched my heart in spray

And the Little Waves of Breffny go stumbling through my soul.

Susan L. Mitchell *(1868 – 1930)*

IMMORTALITY

Age cannot reach me where the veils of God have shut me in,

For me the myriad births of stars and suns do but begin,

And here how fragrantly there blows to me the holy breath,

Sweet from the flowers and stars and hearts of men,

From life and death.

We are not old, O heart, we are not old,

the breath that blows

The soul aflame is still a wandering wind

That comes and goes;

And the stirred heart with sudden raptured life a moment glows.

A moment here – a bulrush's brown head in the grey rain,

A moment there – a child drowned and a heart quickened with pain;

the name of Death, the blue deep heaven, the scent of the salt sea.,

The spicy grass, the honey robbed from the wild bee.

Awhile we walk the world on its wide roads and narrow ways,

And they pass by, the countless shadowy troops of nights and days;

We know them not, O happy heart, for you and I

Watch where within a slow dawn lightens up another sky.

W.B. Yeats *(1865 – 1939)* – two poems

WHEN YOU ARE OLD

When you are old and grey and full of sleep,

And nodding by the fire, take down this book,

And slowly read, and dream of the soft look

Your eyes had once, and of their shadows deep;

Below: Gorteen Bay, Connemara

How many loved your moments of glad grace,

And loved your beauty with love false or true,

But one man loved the pilgrim soul in you,

And loved the sorrows of your changing face;

And bending down beside the glowing bars,

Murmur, a little sadly, how love fled

And paced upon the mountains overhead

And hid his face amid a crowd of stars.

BROKEN DREAMS

There is grey in your hair.

Young men no longer suddenly catch their breath

When you are passing;

But maybe some old gaffer mutters a blessing

Because it was your prayer

Recovered him upon the bed of death.

For your sole sake – that all heart's ache have known

And given to others all heart's ache,

From meagre girlhood's putting on

Burdensome beauty – for your sole sake

Heaven has put away the stroke of her doom,

So great her portion in that peace you make

By merely walking in a room.

Your beauty can but leave among us

Vague memories, nothing but memories

A young man when the old men are done talking

Will say to an old man, "tell me of that lady

the poet stubborn with his passion sang us

When age might well have chilled his blood."

Vague memories, nothing but memories,

But in the grave all, all, shall be renewed,

The certainty that I shall see that lady

Leaning or standing or walking

In the first loveliness of womanhood,

And with the fervour of my youthful eyes,

Has set me muttering like a fool.

You are more beautiful than any one,

And yet your body has a flaw:

Your small hands were not beautiful,

And I am afraid that you will run

And paddle to the wrist

In that mysterious, always brimming lake

Where those that have obeyed the holy law

Paddle and are perfect. Leave unchanged

The hands that I have kissed,

For old sake's sake.

The last stroke of midnight dies.

All day in the one chair

From dream to dream and rhyme to rhyme. I have ranged

In rambling talk with an image of air:

Vague memories, nothing but memories.

James Joyce *(1882 – 1941)*

THE ONDT AND THE GRACEHOPER

He larved ond he larved on he merd such a nauses

The Gracehoper feared he would mixplace his fauces.

I forgive you, grondt Ondt, said the Gracehoper, weeping,

For their sukes of the sakes you are safe in whose keeping.

Teach Floh and Luse polkas, show Bienie where's sweet

And be sure Vespatilla fines fat ones to heat.

As I once played the piper I must now pay the count

So saida to Moyhammlet and marhaba to your Mount!

Let who likes lump above so what flies be a full 'un;

I could not feel moregruggy if this was prompollen.

I pick up your reproof, the horsegift of a friend,

For the prize of your save is the price of my spend.

Can castwhores pulladeftkiss if oldpollocks forsake'em

Or Culex feel etchy if Pulex don't wake him?

A locus to loue, a term it t'embarass,

These twain are the twins that tick *Homo Vulgaris*.

Has Aquileone nort winged to go syf

Since the Gwyfyn we were in his farrest drewbryf

And that Accident Man not beseeked where his story ends

Since longsephyring sighs sought heartseast for their orience?

We were Wastenot with Want, precondamned, two and true,

Till Nolans go volants and Bruneyes come blue.

Below. The Vale of Ovoca, Wicklow

Ere those gidflirts now gadding you quit your mocks for my gropes

An extense must impull, an elapse must elopes,

Of my tectucs takestock, tinktact, and ail's weal;

As I view by your farlook hale yourself to my heal.

Partiprise my thinwhins whiles my blink points unbroken on

Your whole's whercabroads with Tout's trightyright token on.

My in risible universe youdly haud find

Sulch oxtrabeeforeness meat soveal behind.

Your feats end enormous, your volumes immense,

(May the Graces I hoped for sing your Ondtship song sense!),

Your genus its worldwide, your spacest sublime!

But, Holy Saltmartin, why can't you beat time?

Louis MacNeice *(1907 – 1963)*

DOGS IN THE PARK

The precise yet furtive etiquette of dogs

Makes them ignore the whistle while they talk

In circles round each other, one-man bonds

Deferred in pauses of this man-made walk

To open vistas to a past of packs

That raven round the stuccoed terraces

And scavenge at the mouth of Stone Age caves;

What man proposes dog on his day disposes

In litter round both human and canine graves,

Then lifts his leg to wash the gravestones clean,

While simultaneously his eyes express

Apology and contempt; his master calls

And at the last and sidelong he returns,

Part heretic, part hack, and jumps and crawls

And fumbles to communicate and fails.

And then they leave the park, the leads are snapped

On to the spiky collars, the tails wag

For no known reason and the ears are pricked

To search through legendary copse and crag

For legendary creatures doomed to die

Even as they, the dogs, were doomed to live.

Patrick Kavanagh *(1905 – 1967)* – two poems

LOVE SONG

She looked as though she didn't care

He looked as though he didn't care;

Yet I heard by telepathy

The story of a love as rare

As ever trembled in the air.

They must not speak, they were afraid

Of what might happen: she might say

"Excuse me Sir" and turn her head

Should he comment upon the day –

"Nice wheather" in a lover's way.

She could smile as women can

With safety – but he might freeze.

So here the poet sought the plan

Of Dante, Petrarch, – and for these

Mute lovers sang love's mysteries.

A MEMORY

An humble song

Sung in the autumn gloam –

Twas but a childish lay, and yet

I listened, and my eyes were wet.

A winged bird it flew

Across the sky-ie blue,

Below. Kathleen Falls, Ballyshannon

By laughing plane and hill

I hear that lyric still

Though the lyricist has wandered home.

A dream trudges on

Beneath a darkening dome –

But across Time's hoarsely shouting seas

From that far land of memories

It comes to me again

That tender deep refrain

And sorrow steals away.

I know that singer gay

I singing, now at home.

Thomas Kinsella *(1928 –   )* – three poems

BEFORE SLEEP

It is time for bed. The cups and saucers are gathered

And stacked in the kitchen, the tray settled

With your tablets, a glass, a small jug of orange.

Are the window shut, and all the doors locked?

I pass near the desk in my room and stand a minute

Looking down the notes I made this morning.

Yes: tomorrow it might do to begin...

Thunder, whispers far-off among my papers.

The wall opposite is blank but alive

– Standing water over sunken currents.

The currents pursue their slow eddies through the house

Scarcely loosening as yet the objects of our love.

Soon the Falls will thunder, our love's detritus

Slide across the brim seriation, glittering,

And vanish, swallowed into that insane

White roar. Chaos. All battered, scattered.

Yes: in the morning I will put on the cataract,

Give it veins, clutching hands, the short shriek of thought.

FIRST LIGHT

A prone couple still sleeps.

Light ascends like a pale gas

Out of the sea: dawn

Light, reaching across the hill

To the dark garden. the grass

Emerges, soaking with grey dew.

Inside, in silence, an empty

Kitchen takes form, tidied and swept,

Blank with marriage – where shrill

Lover and beloved have kept

Another vigil far

Into the night, and raved and wept.

Upstairs a whimper or sigh

Comes from an open bedroom door

And lengthens to an ugly wail

– A child enduring a dream

That grows, at the first touch of the day,

Unendurable.

SOFT TOY

I am soiled with the repetition of your loves and hatreds

And other experiments. You do not hate me,

Crumpled in my corner. You do not love me,

A small heaped corpse. My face of beaten fur

Responds as you please: if you do not smile

It does not smile: to impatience or distaste

It answers blankness, beyond your goodwill

– Blank conviction, beyond your understanding or mine

I lie limp with use and re-use, listening.

Loose ends of conversations, hesitations,

Half-beginnings that peter out in my presence,

Are enough. I understand, with a flame of shame

Or a click of ease or joy, inert. Knowledge

Into resignation: the process drives deeper,

Grows clearer, eradicating chance growths of desire

– And colder: all possibilities of desire.

My mutton-brown hard eyes fix your need

To grow, as you crush me with tears and throw aside.

Below. Hill of Howth and Ireland's Eye

Most they reflect, but something absorbs – brightening

In response, with energy, to the energy of your changes.

Clutched tightly through the night, held before you.

Ragged and quietly crumpled, as you thrust, are thrust,

In dull terror into your opening brain,

I face the dark with eyes that cannot close

– The cold, outermost points of your will, as you sleep.

Between your tyrannous pressure and the black

Resistance of the void my blankness hardens

To a blunt probe, a cold pitted grey face.

John Montague *(1929 –   )*

THAT ROOM

Side by side on the narrow bed

We lay, like chained giants,

Tasting each other's tears, in terror

Of the news which let little to hide

But our two faces that stared

To ritual masks, absurd and flayed.

Rarely in a lifetime comes such news

Shafting knowledge straight to the heart

Making shameless sorrow start –

Not childish tears, querulously vain –

But adult tears that hurt and harm,

Seeping like acid to the bone.

Sound of hooves on the midnight road

Raised a dramatic image to mind:

The Dean riding late to Marley?

But he must suffer the facts of self;

And no one will ever know

What happened in that room

But when we came to leave

We scrubbed each other's tears

Prepared the usual show. That day

Love's claims made chains of time and place

To bind us together more: equal in adversity.

Brendan Kennelly *(1936 –   )* – two poems

THE THROW

The stone was round and smooth in the boy's hand.

Balanced in his own silence

The silence of summer wrapping him round

He threw the stone over the ruined castle

Rooted in proven ground.

The stone soared and dropped like a shot bird

Into the river

He couldn't see where it fell

But felt the ripples in his mind

Speaking out from the deep centre

Towards the four margins of the water.

Small blue flowers crouched among the reeds,

Brothers and sisters

Hiding behind curtains of silence

When a strange man

Strode into the house

Giant words from his mouth

Tumbling out and down

Like waterfalls

To boom

And drown

The house

And everyone there

Whose life was the throw of a stone.

LEAVING

Relihan stood at the door of the council house,

Muttered 'Now is no time for grieving;'

Below. A watery sunset, Lough Leane, Killarney

Wife and children stared into his face

Refusing to believe he was leaving

Them for good. His hand circled the dull knob

Of the door between him and anonymity,

Heart hardening to each broken sob

Stabbing the air. Already he could see

Strangers in the eyes begging him to stay,

More strange to him than all that lay unknown

In the deep adventure of England.

He looked at his own for the last time, turned away

From the warm squalor of home.

Worlds died, were born in the turn of his hand.

❧❧

Seamus Heaney *(1939 –   )* – three poems

THE RAIN STICK (for Bell and Rand)

Upend the rain stick and what happens next

Is a music that you never would have known

To listen for. In a cactus stalk.

Downpour, sluice-rush, spillage and back wash

Come flowing through. You stand there like a pipe

Being played by water, you shake it again lightly

And diminuendo runs through all its scales
Like a gutter stopping trickling. And now here comes
A sprinkle of drops out of the freshened leaves,

Then subtle little wets off grass and daisies;
Then glitter-drizzle, almost breaths of air.
Upend the stick again. What happens next

Is undiminished for having happened once,
Twice, ten, a thousand times before.
Who cares if all the music that transpires

Is the fall of grit or dry seeds through a cactus?
You are like a rich man entering heaven
Through the ear of a raindrop. Listen now again.

FOLLOWER

My father worked with a horse-plough,
His shoulders globed like a full sail strung
Between the shafts and the furrow.
The horses strained at his clicking tongue.

An expert. He would set the wing
And fit the bright steel-pointed sock.

The sod rolled over without breaking.

At the headrig, with a single pluck

Of reins, the sweating team turned round

And back into the land. His eye

Narrowed and angled at the ground,

Mapping the furrow exactly.

I stumbled in his hobnailed wake,

Fell sometimes on the polished sod

Sometimes he rode me on his back

Dipping and rising to his plod.

I wanted to grow up and plough,

To close one eye, stiffen my arm.

All I ever did was follow

In his broad shadow round the farm.

I was a nuisance, tripping, falling,

Yapping always. But today

It is my father who keeps stumbling

Behind me, and will not go away.

THE FORGE

All I know is a door into the dark.

Outside, old axles and iron hoops rusting;

Inside, the hammered anvil's short pitched ring,

The unpredictable fantail of sparks

Or hiss when a new shoe thoughens in water.

Below. Dunluce Castle, Giant's Causeway

The anvil must be somewhere in the centre,

Horned as a unicorn, at one end square,

Set there immoveable: an altar

Where he expends himself in shape and music.

Sometimes, leather-aproned, hairs in his nose,

He leans out on the jamb, recalls a clatter

Of hoofs where traffic is flashing in rows;

Then grunts and goes in, with a slam and flick

To beat real iron out, to work the bellows.